Christmas Conversations

Jenneth Graser

Jenneth Graser

© **2019 Jenneth Graser**

Secret Place Devotion Publishing

Cover Design – Jenneth Graser
Photography – Adam Chang

First edition – December 2019

www.secretplacedevotion.weebly.com

I dedicate this book with love to Bob and Elizabeth Holmes, whose courage inspires the hearts of many.

Dear Friend,

I invite you to enter the sanctuary of Advent through a series of love notes.

May you be caught up in your own Christmas conversations, where Christ is born anew within you, body, mind and spirit.

With love and blessings,
Jenneth

That night,
in a field near Bethlehem,
there were shepherds
watching over their flocks.

Suddenly,
an angel of the Lord appeared
in radiant splendour before them,
lighting up the field
with the blazing glory of God,
and the shepherds were terrified!

Luke 2:8-9

My Child,

It is time to lay all things aside.
To step into Spirit.
Let me wash the grief of unfinished business
out of your heart.
Listen to the gasp of humble shepherds
in a moment called *suddenly*.
Something is about to begin.

My Lord,

I watch and wait for your coming.

My Child,

It is not a matter of many words.
It is a meeting place where your destiny
aligns with my calling.
I am calling. Do you hear?
All is quiet and completely unexpected and *suddenly*
the shepherd's faces reflect the light
of angels and heavenly song.
Something is about to begin.
Do you hear it?

Lord,

I come to encounter you.
I make my heart ready for your coming.
I open my spirit to hear.

But the angel reassured them, saying,
"Don't be afraid.
For I have come
to bring you good news,
the most joyous news
the world has ever heard!
And it is for everyone
everywhere!

For today in Bethlehem
a rescuer was born
for you.
He is the Lord Yahweh,
the Messiah."

Luke 2:10-11

My Child,

Come up here.
Let us together watch the story
as it unfolds.
Find yourself among the faces of shepherds,
glistening with holiness and a great unknowing.
Watch and wait with me
for what is about to come.
I will always surprise you
with wonder.

Lord,

I can almost hear it now.
And I receive.
You will come to me
and I will feel it all over again,
the wonder
of the Christmas story.

My Child,

When you listen to the Christmas story,
you will hear it with new ears.
When you read the words you know by heart,
I will fill you with wonder.
You are not going to strive your way
into my presence.
You are here.
I am here.

Lord,

Too often I have turned aside
instead of finding you where you
have always promised to be.
I come to your living word
and read the age old story of your coming.
I am there, following the singing of angels,
the light of a star
and the voice of my Father.
I have come
to the place of your arrival.
I have made my heart,
a place for you to rest.

You will recognise him
by this miracle sign:
You will find a baby
wrapped in strips of cloth
and lying in a feeding trough!"

Then all at once,
a vast number of glorious angels appeared,
the very armies of heaven!
And they all praised God, singing:

"Glory to God
in the highest realms of heaven!
For there is peace
and good hope
given to the sons of men."

Luke 2:12-14

My Child,

Look underneath the layers of story
and you will find wisdom waiting
for you in a personal way.
Prepare yourself
for the greatest wonders of your life.
The old is passing away.
The new is about to come.
I do not disappoint
the ones who position
themselves in my heart.
My heart is not a place
of disappointment.
I lift the pressure.
I melt the depression
off of your life.
I ease the burden.
I remove the weight of the world.
I hold the questions.
I am not afraid of your questions.

Lord,

You are too faithful for me to
ever fully understand.
No matter how old I feel inside,
you are able to make all things new.

My Child,

So much is yet to come.
But for now, pause at the
movements of our deeper story.
The treasure is hidden
for you.
My treasure is hidden
in you.

Lord,

I will quiet myself
and watch the story
unfold.
I will live into the story
with your Spirit
to guide
the way.

When the choir of angels
disappeared back to heaven,
the shepherds said to one another,
"Let's go! Let's hurry and find this Word
that is born in Bethlehem
and see for ourselves
what the Lord has revealed to us."

Luke 2:15

My Child,

Get ready for me.
Open your hands to receive.
Awaken your heart.
Be alert to my coming.
You will not miss it.
I will not pass you by.
I am here.

Jenneth Graser

Lord,

Even the familiar scenes
will become extraordinary to me.
Even the hymns of a thousand generations
will sound new to my ears.
I will soften into the moment
of your coming.
I am the one
through which you will come.

My Child,

Let us contemplate together
the year that has passed.
Allow for time to reflect upon
what has gone before.
I want to speak to you through the signs,
patterns, and messages of my Spirit
in the living of life
as it has been.

Lord,

You alone know.
You alone see.
Allow me to recognise the signs of your coming.
I will ponder with you
over what has been,
before we look together
at what is,
and what is yet to come.

So they ran into the village
and found their way
to Mary and Joseph.
And there was the baby,
lying in a feeding trough.

Upon seeing this miraculous sign,
the shepherds recounted
what had just happened.
Everyone who heard the shepherds' story
was astonished by what they were told.

Luke 2:16-18

Jenneth Graser

My Child,

You can cultivate a place
of humble comings
every day of your waking hours.
As you turn the light of your eyes
into my face, I see you.

Lord,

I will cherish every time your hand
has moved within my days.
I will be intentional
about a simple life.
You are changing the settings of my heart,
so that distractions do not set the tone.
It is through quiet joys
and the movements of nature,
it is through the faces of the ones I love
that you have come.

My Child,

I have promised to never leave you alone.
My friendship is your mainstay.
You can be assured of my presence,
whether you feel it or not.
As you embrace the truth
of my presence,
always here,
you will grow in gratitude
and wonder.

Lord,

I have listened to the voices
of the many.
Now I position my heart
in the silence.
My circumstances have at times
swayed my faith and belief.
But you have been to me
a dove on my shoulder.
You have always sent
a promise.

But Mary
treasured all these things
in her heart
and often pondered
what they meant.

Luke 2:19

My Child,

Your mind is not conditioned
by circumstance, but by promise.
I am holding you by the hand
and my support is gentle
and yet constant.
I have walked with you
through all things.
I walk with you now
and I will be in step with you
throughout the new year.

Jenneth Graser

Lord,

Allow for me to express,
my thanks.
Allow for me to pour out
what has been,
so that your living waters
may flow through me
and wash all of the stale
and old happenings
away.

My Child,

Blessed are you.
I bless you with my eyes.
My words do not return void.
I fill my words with the essence of my life.
I breathe through your mind
a new habitation of my living word.
Follow the star to the place of my coming.

Lord,

I make my heart ready.
You enjoy surprises.
You do not mind arriving
in ways that expand the thoughts,
and yet delight the heart.
Your humility
is always my guide.
Come to me Jesus.
Come to me Christ.
Be born in me with what is new
and yet old.
Be born in me with wonder
and resurrection.

The shepherds returned to their flock,
ecstatic over what had happened.
They praised God
and glorified him
for all they had heard
and seen for themselves,
just like the angel
had said.

Luke 2:20

My Child,

My whispers are louder
than the many voices of the world.
My strength is greater
than the empty promises
that fail to deliver.
You have turned to the right
and to the left
and yet you have heard my voice.
It is ok to come to me with doubt.
It is ok to come to me with questions.
I will come to you in ways
that will make your whole spirit
tremble with awe and joy.

Lord,

It has been a long road
with many diversions,
as well as countless joys.
As I look into the night sky,
your star will guide the way beyond
the clutter of distraction
to the one and only thing
that is needful.
I will come to the manger
and find you.
My heart settles
into listening.

My Child,

I will speak to your spirit.
You are able to hear - far more able
than you have thought or imagined.

Lord,

I give you the offerings of my spirit.
The gold, frankincense and myrrh.
I give to you the tired and lonely places.
I give to you my relationships.
I give you my health and circumstances.
You are determined
to show yourself faithful.
I will see the goodness of God
in the land of the living.

Jenneth Graser

After Jesus' birth
a group of spiritual priests
from the East
came to Jerusalem
and inquired of the people,
"Where is the child
who is born king
of the Jewish people?
We observed his star
rising in the sky
and we've come to bow
before him in worship."

Matthew 2:1-2

My Child,

You are so right.
You will see my goodness.
Not always in the ways you hope for or expect,
but in even better ways.
My ways are not your ways,
neither are my thoughts your thoughts.
And yet, you have the mind of Christ.
Yes, you are seated with me
in the posture of your spirit
in heavenly realms.
I shape every frustration,
in the same way a potter turns clay,
into vessels of possibility.
I shape the weakness of your heart
into fruit that remains.

Lord,

I see in you a hope
that outlasts.
I see in you a courage
that responds.
I hear in you a worship
that extends
far beyond my circumstances.
I receive from you
hope and courage.
I give to you,
my worship.

My Child,

Turn your eyes
away from the longings
and desires you have,
that are as yet unfulfilled.
Turn into my presence.
Look up.

Lord,

You are so right.
It is always honesty
and transparency
that make me feel
so much closer to you.
I can say it as it is.
And always,
you remain true.

...and on their way
to Bethlehem,
suddenly the same star
they had seen in the East
reappeared!

Amazed,
they watched as it went
ahead of them
and stopped
directly over the place
where the child was.

And when they saw the star,
they were so ecstatic
that they shouted
and celebrated
with unrestrained joy.

Matthew 2:9-10

Jenneth Graser

My Child,

I am not astonished
by the frailty of your humanity.
Remember,
it is in the frailty of humanity
that I arrived.
And your eternity
is bound up
in the eternity of my love.

Lord,

Your wisdom will continue
to confound me.
And yet you make yourself
known to the children and animals.
I will kneel into the gentle power
of your coming.
And your offerings of time
are abundant.
Always here for me,
no matter the season,
the day or the hour.

My Child,

Prepare the way.
Make the paths clear,
build up the highways
clear the obstacles out of the road,
for the Prince of peace
is coming.

Lord,

You breathe through my faith
with a new creation.
You make my spirit
attentive to you like a child,
excited to be alive.
You are generous
towards me in ways
I have as yet to comprehend.
And the old things
will not hinder or hold me back.
The old ways do not determine
the outcome of the way ahead.
You will guide my feet
in the paths of peace.

Jenneth Graser

When they came
into the house
and saw the young child
with Mary, his mother,
they were overcome.

Falling to the ground at his feet
they worshiped him.
Then they opened
their treasure boxes full of gifts
and presented him with
gold, frankincense, and myrrh.

Matthew 2:11

My Child,

I will light up the year
one step at a time.
I am the God of sudden
changes.
And also the God of slow,
deep movements.
As you align yourself
with my rhythms and seasons,
time will feel light
and sacred.
I have set eternity
in your heart
for a reason.

Lord,

You have fashioned patience
where there has been a lack of it.
Your timing will not be
a point of contention.
I will not wrestle with you
until the day breaks.
I will cease striving
and remain.
I will cease trying
to make things happen,
and wait on the miracles
that flow from your hand.
I will receive the name
you have for me.

My Child,

My love is your constant.
I sing over your life
a love that remains.
My eyes
are alive with miracles
of love everlasting.
The impossible things
are not impossible
to God.

Lord,

It is never too late.
In fact,
it is always the perfect time
to experience the joy
of your coming.

Not one promise from God
is empty of power,
for nothing is impossible
with God!

Luke 1:37

My Child,

I am the author and perfecter
of your faith.
I am the provider of mustard seeds
for the planting.
I am the one who believes
and imparts faith.
I create something
out of nothing.

Lord,

I celebrate you
in ways that are completely
out of the box.
You are forming something new in me
that I have yet to explore.
Let this Christmas glory
shine out of my life
into each and every day
of the year to come.
I will not miss
what you have planned
for my life.

My Child,

Yes, you cannot miss what I am about to do.
I remove the anxiety and worry from your life.
I replace it with transcendent grace.
I give you peace that goes beyond
what your mind can figure out.
You will not be able to think your way
into the future I have in store for you.
I have plans to prosper and not to harm you.
This is my promise.

Lord,

I will keep in pace
with your Spirit.
I will step out into the
impossible places.
I will dream with you -
impossible dreams.
We will walk on the water
of new beginnings.

For the Light of Truth
was about to come
into the world
and shine upon everyone.

John 1:9

My Child,

I am born
through your life.
Every time you share in my story,
every time you share in my love,
every time you take a breath
on this world
of my making,
I am born
through your life.

Lord,

Take me deeper into your story.
I love you.

◆ ◆ ◆

My Child,

Let us write this story
together.
I love you.

He entered
into the very world
he created,
yet the world was unaware.

He came
to the very people
he created –
to those who should have
recognised him,
but they did not receive him.

But those
who embraced him
and took hold
of his name
were given authority
to become
the children of God!

John 1:10-12

About the Author

Jenneth has her poetry published with Tiferet Journal and she is part of a community of writers for the Godspace blog. Her poetry has appeared in Women's Spiritual Poetry Blog and My Utmost Christian Writers. She is the author of Catching the Light, The Present Moment of Happiness and Prayers for a Pioneer.

Jenneth lives in the seaside valley of Hout Bay in the Western Cape of South Africa with her husband, Karl and three daughters. She is a writer and homeschool parent. Karl and Jenneth have a deep desire to see people work together in unity to overcome obstacles and make the changes in their communities fuelled by love and to see the walls between people come down.

Through her writing, Jenneth has a desire to share hope, the ability to dream again, believe in miracles, learn to love yourself unconditionally as a healing path towards loving others, embrace your own personal power, live into the fullness of your destiny, forgive well and learn to live in the present moment with a grateful spirit, as these are all areas of ongoing growth and transformation in her own life. Jenneth is a firm believer in the fact that we never arrive, but are always changing, learning and growing – even into eternity.

Printed in Great Britain
by Amazon

22747760R00040